# NEW ORLEANS
# CLASSICS

## PIANO

MUSIC MINUS ONE

6030

# SUGGESTIONS FOR USING THIS MMO EDITION

WE HAVE TRIED to create a product that will provide you an easy way to learn and perform these compositions with a full ensemble in the comfort of your own home. Because it involves a fixed accompaniment performance, there is an inherent lack of flexibility in tempo. The following MMO features and techniques will reduce these inflexibilities and help you maximize the effectiveness of the MMO practice and performance system:

We have observed generally accepted tempi, and always in the originally intended key, but some may wish to perform at a different tempo, or to slow down or speed up the accompaniment for practice purposes; or to alter the piece to a more comfortable key. We have included slow-tempo versions of the most up-tempo pieces on this album for practice and/or a slower interpretation. But for even more flexibility, you can purchase from MMO specialized CD players & recorders which allow variable speed while maintaining proper pitch, and vice versa. This is an indispensable tool for the serious musician and you may wish to look into purchasing this useful piece of equipment for full enjoyment of all your MMO editions.

We want to provide you with the most useful practice and performance accompaniments possible. If you have any suggestions for improving the MMO system, please feel free to contact us. You can reach us by e-mail at info@musicminusone.com.

6030

# CONTENTS

ISBN 1-59615-115-3

# PREFACE

Here are some general ideas about playing traditional jazz piano in a jazz band.

1. Listen to as many recordings as you can. Check out not only Jelly Roll Morton and the great stride masters (James P. Johnson, Fats Waller, Willie "The Lion" Smith), but also the people they influenced. In Morton's case, this would be Butch Thompson, Don Ewell and others; the more modern stride masters include Ewell, Dick Hyman, Dick Wellstood, Louis Mazetier, Johnny Guarnieri and Ralph Sutton.

2. Learn to distinguish between the many styles lumped together as "traditional jazz": Classic New Orleans Jazz, Dixieland, the New Orleans Revival, West Coast. Knowing what style your band leader likes will help you play appropriately, that is to say, with the right chord voicings and the right rhythmic approach.

3. The biggest mistake pianists make in a trad jazz situation is overplaying, and I've been as guilty of this as anybody. At the very least, make sure you are playing fewer notes per bar than the soloist you are backing! Your job is to support the soloist, not to draw attention away from him or her.

4. Another problem is playing in the same register as the soloist. Be conscious of when a horn player is playing in a lower or upper register and stay out of his way; comp high when the notes are low (as when a bass player is soloing) and low when the horns are screeching.

5. If you're going to play stride piano in a band, make sure you and the bass player are in sync; a good bass player will be able to pick up the patterns you play with your left hand and react accordingly. I've heard bands where the bass, piano and banjo were all playing different chord changes! This comes from not listening, an easy trap to fall into if you're playing the same 100 tunes over and over.

6. Try and find the original recording of any tune you play. You don't have to play the tune this way, but it's good to have the original as a reference point. The more versions of a particular song you can draw from, the richer your version can be.

7. Learn to riff. Utilize breaks creatively. Learn to play all tunes you know in two keys, and slip in solos in the different keys (but tell the bass player first!). Relax, be creative and have fun.

‡

Here are some notes on the included piano sample choruses that you may find helpful:

*Blue Orleans:* The arrangement here exploits the I-IV-I gospel sound.

*Dumaine Street Breakdown:* The solo I've written here is built off a famous lick by Alphonse Picou that is now part of most performances of "High Society."

*Savoy Blues:* A little boogie-woogie, with a simple left-hand pattern.

*Someday You'll Be Sorry:* This song is played with different sets of changes by different people. Here is one common set of changes.

—*Tom McDermott*

Piano

# Fidgety Feet

Original Dixieland Jazz Band

SOLO CHORUS-PLAY 12 TIMES
CLARINET 2Xs- CORNET 2Xs
SAX 2Xs-TROMBONE 2Xs
PIANO 2Xs-BASS & DRUM DUET 2Xs

8

PIANO

# Fidgety Feet
## Piano Sample Chorus

Original Dixieland Jazz Band

# Tin Roof Blues
## Piano Sample Chorus

New Orleans Rhythm Kings

# Tin Roof Blues

New Orleans Rhythm Kings

PIANO

# Royal Garden Blues

Clarence & Spencer Williams

13

# Royal Garden Blues

## Piano Sample Chorus

CLARENCE & SPENCER WILLIAMS

# Blue Orleans
## Two Piano Sample Choruses

PIANO

Tim Laughlin

MMO 6030

PIANO

# Blue Orleans

TIM LAUGHLIN

# Dumaine Street Breakdown

Tim Laughlin

PLAY SIX TIMES-ENSEMBLE 2Xs-CLARINET 1X-CORNET 1X-SAX 1X -TROMBONE 1X

# Dumaine Street Breakdown

## Sample Piano Solo

TIM LAUGHLIN

PIANO

# Savoy Blues
## Piano Sample Chorus

Edward "Kid" Ory

MMO 6030

PIANO

# Savoy Blues

Edward "Kid" Ory

Piano

# March of the Uncle Bubbys

Tim Laughlin

DIXIELAND BAND ENSEMBLE-PLAY TWO TIMES

PLAY FIVE TIMES

CLARINET 1X--CORNET 1X--SAXOPHONE 1X
TROMBONE 1X--CLARINET-TROMBONE DUET 1X

PIANO

# March of the Uncle Bubbys

## Sample Piano Solo

Tim Laughlin

MMO 6030

# Do You Know What It
# Means to Miss New Orleans?

### Piano Sample Chorus

PIANO

Eddie DeLang
Louis Alter

MMO 6030

# Do You Know What It Means to Miss New Orleans?

Eddie DeLang
Louis Alter

**Piano**

# Someday You'll Be Sorry

# Someday You'll Be Sorry

## Piano Sample Chorus

Louis Armstrong

PIANO

# Quincy Street Stomp

## Piano Sample Chorus

SIDNEY BECHET

MMO 6030

PIANO

# Quincy Street Stomp

Sidney Bechet

**MUSIC MINUS ONE**
50 Executive Boulevard
Elmsford, New York 10523-1325
1.800.669.7464 (U.S.)/914.592.1188 (International)

www.musicminusone.com
e-mail: mmogroup@musicminusone.com